British Library Cataloguing in Publication Data. A catalogue record for this book is available from the British Library.

Published by Eagle, an imprint of Inter Publishing Service (IPS) Ltd, PO Box 530, Guildford, Surrey GU2 5FH.

Designed by Roger Judd
Typeset by Eagle
Printed in India
ISBN No: 0 86347 353 9

A PANORAMA OF THE BIBLE LANDS

Text by Stephen Sizer

Photographs by Jon Arnold

eagle

Guildford, Surey

Contents

A VIEW OF EGIRDIR LAKE, PISIDIAN ANTIOCH

PREFACE . . . . JOHN STOTT 5

INTRODUCTION, STEPHEN SIZER ... 7

BETHLEHEM 8

CANA 12

CAPERNAUM 16

HILLS OF GALILEE 20

CAESAREA PHILIPPI 24

WESTERN WALL 28

THE MOUNT OF OLIVES 32

ST PETER IN GALICANTU 36

PISIDIAN ANTIOCH 40

PERGAMUM 44

SARDIS 48

COLOSSE 52

EPHESUS 56

ATHENS 64

CORINTH 68

ROME 72

MEGIDDO & THE JEZEREEL VALLEY ... 76

APPENDIX 80

Foreword

THE HOLY
SEPULCHRE,
JERUSALEM

After the success of Stephen Sizer's first book, *A Panorama of the Holy Land,* this sequel (which reaches further into the Mediterranean and Middle East) is sure to attract a wide readership. *A Panorama of the Bible Lands* might well have borrowed the title of a well known 19th Century volume by George Adam Smith entitled *The Historical Geography of the Holy Land.* For it is a fine blend of history, geography, biblical allusion and Christian teaching.

Like the ripples caused by a bird landing on water, we are taken on a journey outward from Palestine, following the Apostles as they are commissioned by the risen Christ and empowered by the Holy Spirit to be his witnesses in the major cities of the Roman empire including Ephesus, Pergamum, Colosse, Corinth, Athens and Rome.

The text itself is long enough to be satisfying and yet brief enough to be accessible to the reader. Its contemporary applications are always relevant and often challenging. It has always been a salutary exercise for the Christian Church in each generation to compare itself with the early Church. Stephen not only draws out the relevant historical and biblical significance of each site, but seeks to highlight its contemporary relevance also. We are reminded, as the New Testament proclaims, that we believe in both the historical Jesus who lived and the contemporary Jesus who lives.

Bible students will enjoy looking up its many references. Would-be pilgrims will use it to prepare for their visit. Those who have already been will be helped to re-live their experience. And those who will never have the chance to go will be able, through the descriptive text and stunning pictures, to imagine the scenes whose names are so familiar. Particularly striking are the 20 or so double-page full colour spreads which occur every few pages and give us spectacular panoramic views.

Luke ends the Acts of the Apostles confidently with Paul preaching, *"boldly and without hindrance"* symbolising the wide open door for the gospel (Acts 28:31). In that sense it is an unfinished book. Although some of the places described here are no longer known for their living Christian presence owing to persecution, it is our privilege to step into their shoes and to make Christ known in our generation. May this book remind you of our heritage and inspire you to fulfil our high calling.

John Stott
May 2000

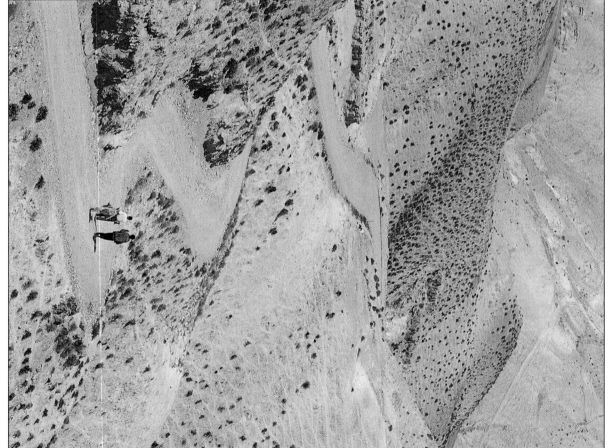

JUDEAN DESERT APPROACHING JERICHO

Introduction

A VIEW OF
THE PROMISED
LAND FROM
MOUNT NEBO

C hristianity is first and foremost a historical faith. It is not primarily a philosophy or an ethical code but is based on the person of Jesus Christ. In this book you are introduced to the most important geographical locations associated with Jesus, from his birth in Bethlehem, through his ministry in Galilee, to his death and resurrection in Jerusalem.

Secondly, Christianity is a missionary faith. After his resurrection Jesus Christ sent out his apostles to go into all the world and make disciples, teaching them to obey all he had commanded them. This book takes you on that journey of faith, tracing the steps of Paul and the other disciples recorded in the Acts of the Apostles. We witness how the first disciples systematically shared the good news of Jesus Christ in each major town and city of the Roman Empire until they finally reached the very heart of Rome itself.

Thirdly, Christianity is a living faith. Whether or not you are already a Christian, reflect on each location and read the biblical references offered to dig deeper into the Scriptures. See how God has used each place within his providential purposes to reveal his love for you also. Discover how Jerusalem, Ephesus, Corinth, Athens, Rome and each of the other sites visited has an abiding message for you today. My prayer is that through this Panorama of the Bible Lands, and its stunning photographs, you may develop a deeper love for the Holy One who came to earth to die for you and rose that you might live for ever. But don't let it stop with you, pass it on!

Stephen Sizer

7

Bethlehem

In those days Caesar Augustus issued a decree that a census should be taken of the entire Roman world. (This was the first census that took place while Quirinius was governor of Syria.) And everyone went to his own town to register. So Joseph also went up from the town of Nazareth in Galilee to Judea, to Bethlehem the town of David, because he belonged to the house and line of David. (Luke 2:1–4)

Originally called Ephrath, meaning 'fruitful' (Genesis 35:16-19), Bethlehem itself means 'house of bread' and it is not hard to see why. Situated about 8 kilometres south of Jerusalem and 750 metres above sea level, Bethlehem commands a strategic location on a ridge running north–south along the watershed of the Judean highlands; dividing the barren desert wilderness of the Jordan Valley to the east from the fertile coastal plain to the west. The slopes on this western side towards Beit Jala abound with figs, almonds, olives and they are still renowned for their vineyards. To

BETHLEHEM STREET

VIEW OVER BETHLEHEM FROM THE CHURCH OF THE NATIVITY

the north lies the traditional site of the shepherds' fields and the tomb of Rachel, Jacob's beloved wife who died in childbirth (Genesis 35:19; 48:7). To the east are the fields associated with the romantic story of Ruth and Boaz, great-grandparents of David (Ruth 1; 2:4; 4:11). Nearby, to the south, is the ancient road from Jerusalem to Hebron and Egypt.

In the Old Testament, Bethlehem is best remembered as the 'City of David'. It was his family home (1 Samuel 16:1; 17:12) and the place where Samuel anointed David to be king of Israel in place of Saul (1 Samuel 16:4-13). Although David eventually made Jerusalem his capital, he never lost his first love for Bethlehem as is seen in the moving story of how three of his brave men risked their lives to obtain water for him from the well in Bethlehem (2 Samuel 23:13-17). In Jeremiah's day the caravansarai near Bethlehem was apparently the usual starting place for travellers to Egypt (Jeremiah 41:17). The inn mentioned in Luke 2 may have possibly been the same one. Following their exile in Babylon only 123 men returned to live in Bethlehem (Ezra 2:21). However, the prophet Micah predicted an even more glorious future because one greater than David, indeed the Saviour of the world, eternal in origin and universal in significance, would also be born there. *'But you, Bethlehem Ephrathah, though you are small among the clans of Judah, out of you will come for me one who will be ruler over Israel, whose origins are from of old, from ancient times . . . his greatness will reach to the ends of the earth'* (Micah 5:2–4).

The New Testament records in great simplicity and humility how that amazing prophecy came true in the lowly birth of the Son of God (Matthew 2; Luke 2; John 7:42). The traditional and undisputed site is found in a cave beneath what is now probably the oldest surviving church in the world, the Church of the Nativity in Manger Square. The tragic fulfillment of another prophecy is remembered nearby in a chapel dedicated to the little boys murdered by Herod in his mad and futile attempt to kill the legitimate King of the Jews (Jeremiah 31:15; Matthew 2:16–18). The bleak and weathered hills on which the lowly shepherds encountered the heavenly angels that first Christmas, though ravaged by centuries of military occupation and human suffering, continue to bear silent witness to our world's desperate need of redemption, of a Saviour who is Christ the Lord.

Even without the snow, Bethlehem is Christmas and Christmas is Bethlehem. However far we wander from the profound simplicity of that first Christmas, however much we become distracted by the materialistic counterfeit, the simple, earthy reality of Bethlehem

brings us back, back to the meaning of Christmas. *'Glory to God in the highest, and on earth peace to men on whom his favour rests'* (Luke 2:14). May you experience that peace today.

SHEPHERDS' FIELDS, BETHLEHEM

BELL TOWER, BETHLEHEM

OLIVE GROVES SOUTH OF BETHLEHEM

Cana of Galilee

'Everyone brings out the choice wine first and then the cheaper wine after the guests have had too much to drink; but you have saved the best till now.' This, the first of his miraculous signs, Jesus performed in Cana of Galilee. He thus revealed his glory, and his disciples put their faith in him. (John 2:10–11)

Cana means *'place of reeds'* suggesting something of the beautiful countryside of lower Galilee. It is distinguished from the other biblical Cana in Lebanon mentioned in Joshua 19 verse 28, by the designation *'Cana of Galilee.'*

Cana survives today as a small town on the tourist road between Nazareth and the Sea of Galilee, just as it was when Jesus took his mother and family and friends 'down' to the lakeside at Capernaum, perhaps for a few day's rest (John 2:12).

Cana was the home of Nathanael, one of the apostles (John 21:2). Although Cana is only mentioned in John's Gospel, it is remembered above all as the place where Jesus performed his first great miraculous 'sign' (John 2:1–11). On another occasion Jesus

BELL TOWER OF THE GREEK CHURCH, CANA

visited the town and encountered a royal official desperate for Jesus to heal his son who was dying. Although Jesus rebukes the people for seeking *'miraculous signs and wonders'* (John 4:48), in compassion and simply by the spoken word, he performs a second miracle in Cana and the boy is healed instantaneously even though he is many miles away in Capernaum.

How appropriate that the divine 'Bridegroom' (Isaiah 62:5; John 3:29; Matthew 9:15), should reveal his glory at a humble wedding. In the days of Jesus, the bridegroom would walk to the house of his bride and they would walk back together to his house followed by their families. The whole town was involved in the procession. When the couple arrived at the groom's house, the reception would take place with plenty of food and wine. Usually the party would last for several days. That is why it was always possible to run out of food or wine. Jesus turned the water into wine, not just to save the couple from embarrassment; it was a sign of what he had come to do for us all.

ROMAN MOSAIC OF WATER CARRIER

come from. Perhaps they too became disciples of Christ, at least after the honeymoon.

Jesus' power to turn water into wine, is a picture of his work in us, the Church, his 'Bride'. Jesus has the power to change our ordinary lives into something special by his presence, his provision and power. The Bible uses the word 'metamorphosis' to describe this amazing transformation (Romans 12:1–2). The 'sign' miracles of Jesus, and this was the first, were not performed to trick or entertain, but to prove that God had come in the person of Jesus to share his joy and love and enable us to know him as our Friend and Saviour.

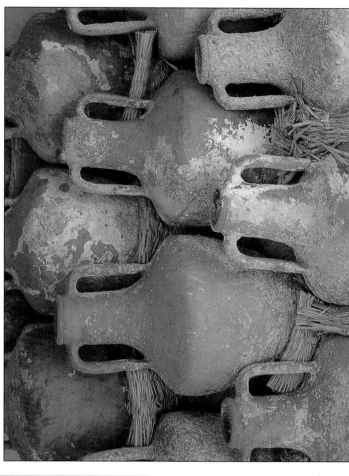

AMPHORAS USED FOR STORING VARIOUS PRODUCTS

FRANCISCAN CHURCH, CANA

Jesus blessed the couple and their community in three specific ways. First he blessed them with his presence, but he needed to be invited. Second, Jesus blessed them with his provision. The six stone water jars held between 120 and 180 gallons which is a lot of wine and it was very good wine at that. Jesus blessed them with quantity and quality, but Mary had to ask him. Third, Jesus blessed them with his power for this was not simply an act of compassion or generosity. It was a supernatural miracle and John points out that as a consequence, *'his disciples put their faith in him'*. I wonder about the bride and groom. They must have also known where the wine had

Capernaum

After Jesus and his disciples arrived in Capernaum… the disciples came to Jesus and asked,'Who is the greatest in the kingdom of heaven?' He called a little child and had him stand among them. And he said,'I tell you the truth, unless you change and become like little children, you will never enter the kingdom of heaven. Therefore, whoever humbles himself like this child is the greatest in the kingdom of heaven. And whoever welcomes a little child like this in my name welcomes me.' (Matthew 17:24, 18:1–5)

SYNAGOGUE, CAPERNAUM

Capernaum is situated on the scenic north-western shore of the Sea of Galilee. This important city, mentioned only in the Gospels, is on the ancient Via Maris, the main international trade route from the Mediterranean coastal plain through the Golan Heights on to Damascus and the East. It is also situated near where the fresh water of the River Jordan, carrying the melted snows of Mount Hermon, enters Galilee. Since the many varieties of fish are attracted to the fresh water, Capernaum came to dominate the thriving fishing communities along the northern shore of this border region, most likely after the return of the Jews from captivity.

This perhaps explains the presence of a Roman tax and customs post as well as a military base under the command of a centurion (Luke 5:27) who also apparently built the synagogue there, the foundations of which are still visible today (Luke 7:1–5). These are probably the reasons why Capernaum is described as a 'city' in the original Greek of the Gospels (Matthew 9:1; Mark 1:21) to distinguish it from the smaller fishing villages nearby such as Bethsaida and Magdala.

STONE
CORNICE (DETAIL)
SYNAGOGUE, CAPERNAUM

mother-in-law (Luke 4:38–39). The scene portrayed by Matthew, Mark and Luke of the whole town gathered at the door of Peter's home, as the sun was going down, is one of the most moving in the New Testament. According to Mark, Jesus continued to minister long after it was dark. *That evening after sunset the people brought to Jesus all the sick and demon-possessed. The whole town gathered at the door . . .* (Mark 1:32–33). Yet his first priority in Capernaum, as elsewhere, was to teach and preach about the kingdom of God (Mark 1:38–39). Although Jesus used Capernaum as his home base, many of the people who lived there did not understand his message and tried unsuccessfully to make him king by force (John 6:14–15).

The message of Capernaum? It is futile trying to make Jesus fit our expectations or our agenda for him. Unless we change and become like little children, we too like those of Capernaum, will never enter the kingdom of heaven (Luke 10:15–16).

STONE CORNICE, CAPERNAUM

CAPERNAUM AND THE SEA OF GALILEE

Capernaum was therefore a strategic location for the development of Jesus' ministry. It was known as the 'Galilee of the Gentiles' (Isaiah 9:1). Matthew sees great significance in this, indeed as the fulfilment of Isaiah's prophecy of the coming Messiah (Matthew 4:13–16). It is not surprising perhaps that when he was rejected in Nazareth Jesus made Capernaum his 'home'. He probably stayed with Peter and his family (Mark 2:1, Luke 4:38–40). Jesus chose several of his disciples from among its residents, including Matthew the tax collector and fishermen such as Simon Peter and his brother Andrew (Matthew 9:9; Mark 1:29).

Jesus frequently taught in the synagogue at Capernaum (Mark 1:21–22; John 6:25–59). Many of his miracles were also performed here, like the healing of the centurion's servant (Matthew 8:5; Luke 7:1–2), the man possessed by a demon (Mark 1:23–28) and Simon's

The Hills of Galilee

When Jesus heard that John had been put in prison, he returned to Galilee. Leaving Nazareth, he went and lived in Capernaum, which was by the lake in the area of Zebulun and Naphtali – to fulfil what was said through the prophet Isaiah: 'Land of Zebulun and land of Naphtali, the way to the sea, along the Jordan, Galilee of the Gentiles – the people living in darkness have seen a great light; on those living in the land of the shadow of death a light has dawned.' (Matthew 4:12–16)

SEA OF GALILEE

G alilee means 'a ring' or 'circuit'. The term is used of the region extending from the Litani River in Lebanon in the north to the Valley of Jezreel in the south, and from the Mediterranean coast in the west to the Jordan River in the east. The region 1,000 metres above sea level is known as Upper Galilee and lies to the north of a line from the Bay of Acco to the Sea of Galilee. In the first century this region was sparsely populated and densely wooded. The region to the south below 1,000 metres above sea level is known as Lower

Galilee and includes the Jezreel Valley. Here the climate is milder, the soil richer and the population was more dense. Josephus says that in the first century there were 204 villages in Galilee.

The first occasion when Galilee appears in the Bible is in the context of 'The king of Goyim in Gilgal' (Joshua 12:23), which may best be translated as 'king of the nations of Galilee'. This reveals the presence of distinct ethnic groups living in Galilee alongside the Israelite tribes of Naphtali, Asher, Issachar and Zebulun, and later, Dan. So, under the monarchy, when Solomon needed to pay Hiram for supplies of wood and gold used in the construction of the temple in Jerusalem, he offered him twenty towns in Galilee as collateral (1 Kings 9:10–14; 2 Chronicles 8:1–2).

About the year 732 BC, Tiglath-Pileser, the king of Assyria, deported the Israelites living in Galilee. He replaced them with people from Babylon and Syria (2 Kings 15:29; 17:24). It is probably for this reason Isaiah describes the area as 'Galilee of the Gentiles', since it was a cosmopolitan mix of Jews, Aramaeans, Ituraeans, Phoenicians and Greeks. It seems Galilee was in some ways a melting pot of different ethnic groups (Isaiah 9:1; Matthew 4:15).

SEA OF GALILEE SEEN FROM THE NORTH

In consequence, Galilee developed a reputation for independence and rebellion against authority (Luke 13:1; Acts 5:37). Galileans also evolved their own distinctive accent (Matthew 26:69, 73) and came to be despised by the more legalistic Jews of Judea in the south. For example, when Nicodemus defended Jesus before the Sanhedrin they replied sarcastically, *'Are you from Galilee, too? Look into it, and you will find that a prophet does not come out of Galilee'* (John 7:52). Their arrogance towards Galileans distorted their historical perspective, for the prophet Jonah, and probably Nahum and Hosea, all came from Galilee.

Dividing Upper from Lower Galilee lies the Sea of Galilee. In the first century the great abundance of fish and shellfish found in the lake attracted a large population in what became a continuous belt of villages along its northern shore. Important fishing towns of more than 15,000 residents included Capernaum and Bethsaida, which means 'house of fish'. Jesus chose Simon Peter and his brother Andrew, together with James and his brother John from among the fishermen of Galilee to be his disciples. In fact all but Judas Iscariot were, like Jesus, from Galilee. He promised they too would become 'fishers of men' (Matthew 4:18–22; Luke 5:1–11). The Sea of Galilee was indeed the cradle of the gospel.

It is most significant, therefore, that Jesus chose to base most of his ministry in Galilee. The hills and villages of Galilee provided a dramatic backdrop for much of the gospel story. Capernaum, for instance, became his home town (Matthew 9:1). Jesus performed his first miracle at the wedding in Cana and his last by the Sea of Galilee (John 2:11; 21:4-12). Indeed twenty-five of his thirty-three recorded miracles were performed here. Likewise nineteen of his thirty-two parables were told in Galilee. This may have been because Galilee gave Jesus access to the rest of the Roman Empire and beyond. Conveniently, the Via Maris, the international highway from Egypt

to Syria, passed along the northern shore near Capernaum. Galilee also enjoyed comparative religious freedom from the priestly and pharisaical legalism and prejudice found in Jerusalem.

Galilee was a microcosm of the world. Jesus made his home there, equipped his disciples and developed his strategy to reach the entire world from the 'Galilee of the Gentiles'. We all live in our own Galilee with its multi-cultural tensions, its ethical challenges and gospel opportunities. Jesus calls us to break down the barriers in our world, overcome our narrow prejudices and share his liberating message in word and deed with everyone we meet, irrespective of their gender, race or culture. Our Lord's words to his first disciples are as much our own mandate too. *'A new command I give you: Love one another. As I have loved you, so you must love one another. By this all men will know that you are my disciples, if you love one another'* (John 13:34–35).

SEA OF GALILEE SEEN FROM THE GOLAN HEIGHTS

HILLS ABOVE THE SEA OF GALILEE

Caesarea Philippi

When Jesus came to the region of Caesarea Philippi, he asked his disciples, 'Who do people say the Son of Man is?' They replied, 'Some say John the Baptist; others say Elijah; and still others, Jeremiah or one of the prophets.' 'But what about you?' he asked. 'Who do you say I am?' Simon Peter answered, 'You are the Christ, the Son of the living God.' Jesus replied, 'Blessed are you, Simon son of Jonah, for this was not revealed to you by man, but by my Father in heaven.' (Matthew 16:13–17)

Caesarea Philippi is situated high up in the Golan Heights on the south-western slope of Mount Hermon, about 190 kilometres from Jerusalem and 80 kilometres from Damascus. It commands a strategic position on the main road through the Golan, dominating the valleys of northern Galilee below. From a cave at the foot of a steep bluff on the northern edge of the city flows one of the two sources of the River Jordan. For these reasons from earliest times, Caesarea Philippi has been a major centre for pagan worship.

Earliest records suggest it was a Canaanite sanctuary and perhaps the site of Baal-Hermon and the worship of the fertility god Baal (Judges 3:3; 1 Chronicles 5:23). A major battle took place here in 198 BC when the Egyptian army was defeated by the Seleucids under Antiochus the Great. During this time of Greek ascendancy in Palestine the site became an important centre for the worship of the god Pan and so was renamed Paneas.

The region eventually fell to the Romans and in 20 BC the emperor Augustus bequeathed Paneas to Herod the Great. Herod built a pagan temple of white marble here dedicated to Augustus Caesar in appreciation of his benefactor. When Herod died, his son Philip became tetrarch and in 4 BC rebuilt the city. He renamed it

ROCK NICHE AT THE TEMPLE TO PAN

BANIYAS SPRING AT THE TEMPLE TO PAN

Caesarea Philippi in deference to Augustus Caesar. He also added his own name to distinguish it from the other Caesarea on the Mediterranean coast. Herod Agrippa II, grandson of Herod the Great, subsequently changed its name to Neronias in honour of the emperor Nero. Still later, having put down the Jewish revolt, the Romans changed the name back to Paneas once again. Today the Syrian village, occupied by Israel since 1967, is known by its Arabic name, Baniyas.

Two niches cut into the face of the rock beside the cave are all that remain of its idolatrous origins. Caesarea Philippi is best remembered, however, as the place where the Lord Jesus Christ was revealed to be the Son of God. Six days after Jesus affirmed Peter's great confession, he was miraculously transfigured, probably nearby on Mount Hermon, meeting with Moses and Elijah, before his stunned disciples, Peter, James and John (Matthew 16:13–17:13). This high and remote region was a most appropriate place for Jesus to take his disciples on retreat to prepare them for his imminent humiliation, crucifixion and, afterwards, his triumphant resur-rection. The transfiguration of Jesus gave a brief glimpse of his true eternal glory, laid aside when he came to earth but restored after his ascension (Philippians 2:5–11). On the basis of Peter's confession that Jesus was the Messiah, it was here in Caesarea Philippi. That Jesus also first revealed his purpose for the Church '...on this rock I will build my church, and the gates of Hades will not overcome it' (Matthew 16:18).

So it was at Caesarea Philippi then that Jesus asked his disciples the most important question they would ever face. 'Who do you say that I am?' It is the same ultimate question we must answer if we too are to be transformed and become like Jesus. 'And we, who with unveiled faces all reflect the Lord's glory, are being transformed into his likeness with ever-increasing glory' (2 Corinthians 3:12–18; Romans 12:1–2).

The Western Wall

O God, the nations have invaded your inheritance; they have defiled your holy temple, they have reduced Jerusalem to rubble.... We are objects of reproach to our neighbours, of scorn and derision to those around us. How long O LORD Will you be angry for ever? How long will your jealousy burn like fire? (Psalm 79:1, 4–5)

David's lament has epitomised the deep feelings and aspirations of Jews down the centuries who have come to the Western or 'Wailing' Wall to pray (Psalm 79:1,4–5). When the temple was destroyed in July AD 70 the Western Wall became the focus of Jewish religious life in Jerusalem. The Hebrew prophets themselves gave an answer to this lament, although their message has not always been welcomed or heeded. *'Rend your heart and not your garments. Return to the LORD your God, for he is gracious and compassionate, slow to anger and abounding in love, and he relents from sending calamity. Who knows? He may turn and have pity and leave behind a blessing...'* (Joel 2:13–14).

The lowest seven courses of stone visible in the Western Wall date back to the Jewish temple built by Herod the Great between 18 BC and AD 28. Below

the pavement level a further nineteen courses reach a depth of 21 metres. Some of these stones which make up the retaining wall of the Temple Mount measure more than 12 metres in length and one is known to weigh 400 tons. The temple walls were constructed so precisely that there was no need for mortar or cement, the stones simply resting one on top of the other. The entire Western Wall of the Temple Mount is 485 metres long although only 57 metres is accessible today. Above the Herodian foundations, the stone work is made up of progressively smaller and smaller stones which date back to the Roman, Muslim and Ottoman periods.

It is possible that the open area adjacent to the Wall today was at the time of Christ an open porticoed plaza used for public gatherings, described by Josephus as the Xystos. It lies on top of some 21 metres of

DOME OF THE ROCK, JERUSALEM

debris built up during the Hellenistic and Roman periods filling in and levelling what was once the Tyropoeon Valley. Archaeology has also revealed that this area was previously the site of a Hellenistic gymnasium built by Jason (2 Maccabees 4:12). Even earlier burial remains discovered here indicate that this area was outside Solomon's walls in the eighth century BC, before the city expanded west.

Jews were prohibited from entering Jerusalem following the destruction of the city in AD 70 and it was not until sometime after the death of Hadrian in 138 that they were allowed to return annually on the 9th July to lament the destruction of the temple. Gradually, as the prohibition was relaxed, Jews began to settle in Jerusalem in small numbers and came to pray near the Temple Mount on other occasions. With the capture of Jerusalem by the Muslims and the construction of shrines on the Temple Mount area, Jews were again denied access and the Western Wall became the nearest location for pilgrimage. For many centuries Jews came here to pray, especially on Friday evenings at the beginning of their Sabbath, to lament the downfall of Jerusalem and the temple. In 1930 the League of Nations declared the area around the Western Wall, known as the Moors' Quarter, to be a Muslim holy place, although the narrow alley adjacent to the Wall remained accessible to Jews for prayer. However, when Israel occupied the city in 1967 they demolished Arab homes and mosques next to the Wall to create the wide plaza now utilised by Jews as a synagogue for prayer, celebrations and bar mitzvah ceremonies.

Today, the Western Wall is a vivid reminder that God no longer dwells in temples made by hands (Acts 17:24). Jesus fulfilled and annulled the role of the temple in the purposes of God. Jesus cleansed the temple which was originally intended to be for all nations (John 2:13–17; Malachi 3:1). He also predicted its destruction because the Jews rejected their Messiah (Matthew 23:37–24:2). Jesus taught that he himself was greater than the temple (Matthew 12:6) and when his authority was questioned, described his body as the temple that mattered (John 2:19). Jesus also taught that the Church would be the new eschatological temple (Matthew 18:19-20; John 14:23) a theme developed by the apostles (1 Corinthians 3:16; 6:19; 2 Corinthians 6:16). By his death Jesus has opened a new way into the presence of God making the Jewish temple unnecessary, a mere fading shadow of the true reality in heaven (Ephesians 2:14–22; Hebrews 8:1-10:18). The New Jerusalem which will one day come down from heaven needs no temple, for we shall see God face to face (Revelation 21:22; 22:4). God's answer therefore to those who still seek him at the Western Wall or even a rebuilt temple may be summarised in Jesus' reply to the Samaritan woman, *'Believe me, woman, a time is coming when you will worship the Father neither on this mountain nor in Jerusalem… Yet a time is coming and has now come when the true worshippers will worship the Father in spirit and truth, for they are the kind of worshippers the Father seeks. God is spirit, and his worshippers must worship in spirit and in truth"* (John 4:21-24).

DOME OF THE ROCK, JERUSALEM

A TORAH AT THE WESTERN WALL

A South-Western View of The Temple Mount

The Mount of Olives

When he came near the place where the road goes down the Mount of Olives, the whole crowd of disciples began joyfully to praise God in loud voices for all the miracles they had seen: "Blessed is the king who comes in the name of the Lord! Peace in heaven and glory in the highest!" (Luke 19:37–38)

OLD CITY FROM THE
MOUNT OF OLIVES

The Mount of Olives is actually a ridge of hills running from north to south for about 4 kilometres to the east of Jerusalem and parallel to the deep ravine of the Kidron Valley. As the name suggests, the hillsides were once covered with dense olive groves. To the east lie the villages of Bethphage and Bethany and beyond them, the Judean wilderness and the Jordan Valley. The barren hills of Moab and the Dead Sea are also visible from this strategic vantage point. For this reason it was known as Jerusalem's watchtower.

The northern end became known as Mount Scopus, meaning 'lookout' because the Roman general Titus used it for his headquarters during the fateful siege of Jerusalem in AD 70. Until the time of Christ, the Mount of Olives had been heavily wooded with many olive trees. These were, however, cut down and used for battering rams and siege machines by the Romans when they destroyed the city. At the southern end where the Kidron

MOUNT OF OLIVES, JERUSALEM

Valley merges with the Valley of Hinnon it is called the Mount of Corruption. Here, where previously the Israelites had worshipped God (2 Samuel 15:30–32), and may have fulfilled the purification ceremony of the red heifer (Numbers 19), King Solomon built 'high places' for 'Ashtoreth the vile goddess of the Sidonians, for Chemosh the vile god of Moab, and for Molech the detestable god of the people of Ammon' (2 Kings 23:13). These were later desecrated by King Josiah who covered the sites with human bones and cut down the Asherah poles to purify the religious practices of Israel (2 Chronicles 34:1–7). Subsequently, the Mount of Olives became associated with the departure of the *shekinah* glory of God from the temple as a sign of Israel's impending exile (Ezekiel 10:18; 11:23).

Parallels between Old and New Testament events which occurred on the Mount of Olives are significant. In the time of Nehemiah, for example, following their return from captivity in Babylon, the Israelites probably gathered branches from the olive trees here, as well as palm branches, to make booths to celebrate the Feast of Tabernacles (Nehemiah 8:15). On what became known as Palm Sunday, the disciples of Jesus similarly gathered branches with which to greet their king as he entered Jerusalem.

Jesus was not the first king of Israel to weep over Jerusalem from the Mount of Olives. When Absalom rebelled against his father David, the deposed king fled the city, his feet bare and head covered in shame. As he looked back over Jerusalem from the Mount of Olives he wept (2 Samuel 15:30–32), even acknowledging that Shimei's curse on him may have been from God (2 Samuel 16:5–10). Centuries later the Lord Jesus wept over Jerusalem from this spot knowing that within days they would call for his crucifixion, rejecting God's way of peace and reconciliation. Jesus would willingly have been cursed in their place but they refused. In tears, Jesus foretold the consequent destruction of Jerusalem as the result of God's judgement upon Israel (Luke 19:41-44).

During the last week of his life Jesus spent much time with his disciples on the Mount of Olives (Mark 13:37; Luke 21:37; 22:39).

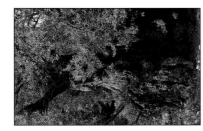

OLD OLIVE TREE, MOUNT OF OLIVES

With its dense foliage and cool evening breezes perhaps it reminded him of Galilee, providing a welcome retreat from the tension of the overcrowded city. Repudiating their mistaken belief that he was still going to restore a physical kingdom to Israel, Jesus commanded them instead to leave Jerusalem and become his witnesses taking the gospel to the whole world. From the Mount of Olives, the Lord physically ascended to heaven, angels promising he would return in the same way (Acts 1:6–12). Zechariah had previously predicted this, indicating that when the Lord Jesus Christ returns to judge the earth, it will be to the Mount of Olives. This dramatic event will be marked by a radical change to its topography. *'On that day his feet will stand on the Mount of Olives, east of Jerusalem, and the Mount of Olives will be split in two from east to west, forming a great valley, with half of the mountain moving north and half moving south'* (Zechariah 14:4).

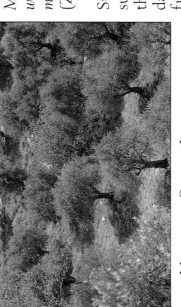

MOUNT OF OLIVES, JERUSALEM

It's easy to be a Christian on Palm Sunday when the sun is shining and we are surrounded by many others worshipping the Lord. It is not so easy on Maundy Thursday when it is dark, we are alone or the future uncertain. Then it is time to remember that it is but a short distance from the Mount of Olives to the Garden of Gethsemane. Before being a place of resurrection and ascension it was first a place of denial and rejection. Ironically the word 'witness' comes from the same word as 'martyr'. For many Christians to be a witness for Christ literally means being a martyr also. Jesus calls us to both (Mark 8:34–38; Acts 1:8–9) and to identify with Paul when he said *'For to me, to live is Christ and to die is gain'* (Philippians 1:21).

Jerusalem from St Peter in Galicantu

'O Jerusalem, Jerusalem, you who kill the prophets and stone those sent to you, how often I have longed to gather your children together, as a hen gathers her chicks under her wings, but you were not willing. Look, your house is left to you desolate. For I tell you, you will not see me again until you say, "Blessed is he who comes in the name of the Lord." ' (Matthew 23:37–39)

4TH CENTURY STEPS
BY ST PETER

The panoramic view of Jerusalem from St Peter in Galicantu is simply stunning. To the left is Mount Zion, traditional site of David's tomb, the Upper Room and the Last Supper. Dominating the view, however, is the south face of the Temple Mount. The enormity of the foundations for this structure are staggering, covering an area of about 35 acres, 446 metres from north to south and 296 metres from east to west. The recently excavated first-century temple steps and bricked-up archway entrance used by Jesus are still visible today. At the south-east corner, originally 45 metres high above the Kidron Valley, stands what many regard as the pinnacle of the temple from where Satan tempted Jesus to throw himself down (Matthew 4:5–7). Behind the temple area, providing a rich green backdrop of olive trees, lies the Kidron Valley and the Mount of Olives. To the right and lower down, are the excavations of David's City, the Pool of Siloam and the Valley of Gehenna which joins the Kidron Valley before beginning its slow, winding descent to the Dead Sea.

The site first gained significance as Mount Moriah because it was here that Abraham was tested over

CHURCH OF ST PETER IN GALICANTU PROBABLY BUILT OVER THE HOUSE OF CAIAPHAS

the sacrifice of Isaac (2 Chronicles 3:1; Genesis 22:1–14). David acquired the hill from Araunah the Jebusite in order to offer a sacrifice to God and save his people (2 Samuel 24:16–25). The privilege of building the temple, however, was given to his son Solomon (1 Kings 5). The remains of the temple walls seen today are actually the third to be built on the site. The first was constructed by Solomon, followed by Zerubbabel, and then Herod. These represent the pre-exilic, post-exilic, and New Testament periods.

The proximity and juxtaposition of the Temple Mount to the Valley of Gehenna is both sobering and profound. *Gehenna* is the Greek for Hinnom and means the 'valley of whining' or 'lamentation'. In the Old Testament it is the place where children were sacrificed to the pagan deities of Baal and Molech (2 Kings 16:3; 17:17; 23:10). Not surprisingly, perhaps, Jesus used the same emotive place to illustrate the eternal reality of hell (Matthew 5:22, 29; 23:15).

The splendid view of Jerusalem from this hilltop encompasses most of the events which occurred in Holy Week. The Last Supper was probably held in the Essene Quarter on what is now Mount Zion, since the disciples were told to follow a man carrying a water pot (Mark 14:13–16). As dusk fell that Maundy Thursday Jesus walked with his disciples over to the Garden of Gethsemane on the Mount of Olives to pray (Luke 22:39–46). There he was arrested by the Jewish religious leaders and brought to the House of Caiaphas for interrogation overnight (Luke 22:47–54). Early on Good Friday he was taken to Pilate, probably in the Antonia Fortress at the north-west corner of the Temple Mount (Luke 23:1–2). After his trial Jesus was led along what is now known as the Via Dolorosa carrying his cross to the place of crucifixion which was then outside the city walls (Matthew 27:27–33). After his death our Lord was placed in a new tomb in a garden nearby (Matthew 27:57–66). Three momentous days later the risen Lord met with the disciples in the Upper Room again before ascending to heaven before their very eyes from the Mount of Olives (John 20:19–31). It is to this same spot that many believe he will return (Acts 1:9–11). This explains the presence of extensive Jewish, Muslim and Christian cemeteries on the slopes of the Kidron Valley and Mount of Olives as all three faiths believe the dead will rise first when the Messiah comes.

This scene then is one of stark contrasts. Calvary, the Mount of Olives and Gehenna. We see in one panoramic view locations associated with both the way to heaven and the path to hell. It is a scene that sums up the heart of our historic credal statements as well as the personal choice before us all. *'See, I set before you today life and prosperity, death and destruction. For I command you today to love the* LORD *your God, to walk in his ways, and to keep his commands, decrees and laws; then you will live and increase, and the* LORD *your God will bless you . . . This day I call heaven and earth as witnesses against you that I have set before you life and death, blessings and curses. Now choose life, so that you and your children may live and that you may love the* LORD *your God, listen to his voice, and hold fast to him'* (Deuteronomy 30:15–16, 19–20)

ST PETER IN GALICANTU

Pisidian Antioch

From Perga they went on to Pisidian Antioch. On the Sabbath they entered the synagogue and sat down. After the reading from the Law and the Prophets, the synagogue rulers sent word to them, saying 'Brothers, if you have a message of encouragement for the people, please speak.' ... As Paul and Barnabas were leaving the synagogue, the people invited them to speak further about these things on the next Sabbath. When the congregation was dismissed, many of the Jews and devout converts to Judaism followed Paul and Barnabas, who talked with them and urged them to continue in the grace of God. On the next Sabbath almost the whole city gathered to hear the word of the Lord. (Acts 13:14–15, 42–44)

Pisidian Antioch was founded by the Selucid king, Seleucus I Nicator around 300 BC. The site is on a plateau close to the west bank of the River Athios, on the edge of the Pisidian Mountains, to the north of Pamphylia and the Taurus Mountains, east of Phrygia and to the west of Lycaonia and Cilicia. The River Athios flows from the Sultan Dagh to the double lake called Egerdir Gol and the area

around Pisidian Antioch is very fertile. The city was named after Nicator's father, Antiochus, as were many others, such as Phrygian Antioch and the Selucid capital of Antioch in Syria (Acts 13:1–3).

The Selucids chose strategic sites such as Pisidian Antioch to control the local tribes and to exploit the great trade route between the Cilician Gates and Ephesus. Xenophon describes how the indigenous people of Pisidia were independent of the kings of Persia from the fifth century BC and that even Alexander the Great had difficulty subjugating these warlike people.

In 189 BC, the Romans declared Pisidian Antioch a 'free city', its citizens no longer were required to pay tribute to the Selucid kings. In 39 BC, Antony gave the city to Amyntas of Galatia and so Pisidian Antioch was transferred to the province of Galatia. The city was made a Roman colony in 6 BC and renamed Caesarea Antiocheia. It became the administrative capital of the province of Galatia and the

ROMAN ACQUEDUCT AT PISIDIAN ANTIOCH

aroused the hostility of the local Jews, threatened by Gentiles coming to faith (Acts 13:48–51). In the region of Pisidia and Phrygia women held positions of wealth and civic office, such as magistrates, and Paul's enemies exploited some of them to ensure he was expelled, but not for long (Acts 13:50). It is likely that this area held a special place in Paul's heart, as his friend and disciple Timothy was from nearby Lystra (Acts 16:1).

Paul visited Pisidian Antioch on each of his missionary journeys (Acts 14:21; 16:6; 18:23) and it is quite possible that it was in this wild and rugged area of Pisidia that he encountered what he describes as, 'danger from bandits . . .' and, 'danger in the country . .' (Acts 14:21–25; 2 Corinthians 11:26).

Pisidian Antioch reminds us that while the human spirit cannot be tamed by external military force but only by Jesus Christ, '. . . everyone who wants to live a godly life in Christ Jesus will be persecuted' (2 Timothy 3:12).

THE THEATRE

most important Roman garrison colony in Asia. Augustus took steps to pacify Pisidia even further by building a network of roads from Pisidian Antioch to five other military colonies at Cremna, Comama, Oblasa, Parlais and Lystra, the latter being called the Royal Road. An inscription has been discovered showing that Quirinius who was governor of Syria at the time of the birth of Christ (Luke 2:2), was also an honorary magistrate of the colony at Pisidian Antioch.

From here the Romans attempted, like the Selucids, to subjugate the rebellious tribes of Pisidia, Isauria and Pamphylia. They imposed Latin as the official language although the discovery of Phrygian inscriptions indicates the cosmopolitan nature of the local population.

It is easy to see why Paul used Psidian Antioch as his base for reaching the region of southern Galatia (Acts 13:49), at least until he

BYZANTINE CHURCH

ROMAN AQUEDUCT, PISIDIAN ANTIOCH

Pergamum

'To the angel of the church in Pergamum write: These are the words of him who has the sharp, double-edged sword. I know where you live – where Satan has his throne. Yet you remain true to my name. You did not renounce your faith in me, even in the days of Antipas, my faithful witness, who was put to death in your city – where Satan lives. Nevertheless, I have a few things against you: You have people there who hold to the teaching of Balaam, who taught Balak to entice the Israelites to sin by eating food sacrificed to idols and by committing sexual immorality. Likewise you also have those who hold to the teaching of the Nicolaitans. Repent therefore! Otherwise, I will soon come to you and will fight against them with the sword of my mouth. He who has an ear, let him hear what the Spirit says to the churches.' (Revelation 2:12–17)

THE ASCLEPION, PERGAMUM

Pergamum is situated on a commanding hill in the Caicus Valley, about five kilometres from the Caicus River, opposite the island of Lesbos, about twenty-four kilometres from the Aegean Sea in north-west Turkey. Although the settlement is known to have been founded well before the fourth century BC, Pergamum rose in prominence after 282 BC when Philetaerus rebelled against Thrace

and made it the capital of the emerging Attalid kingdom in the region of Mysia.

Pergamum came to be seen as a symbol of Greek supremacy over the Barbarians. Besides many fine buildings, the library in Pergamum, for example, grew in size and prestige until it contained over 200,000 volumes and rivalled that of Alexandria. Because of this the Egyptians banned exports of papyrus to Pergamum. Scholars there devised a new material for writing known as *Pergamena charta*, or parchment, named after the city.

THE TEMPLE OF TRAJAN, PERGAMUM

In 133 BC, Attalus III bequeathed the city to the Romans and it became the capital of their province of Asia. Ironically Mark Antony gave Pergamum's library to Cleopatra as a sign of their friendship and its priceless volumes were moved to Alexandria.

The city was also a focus for the worship of four important Greek gods: Zeus, Athena, Dionysus and Aesclepius. Aesclepius was the pagan god of healing and archaeologists have found the hospital complex where sick people from the surrounding region were brought in the hope of finding a cure here.

Pergamum is the third city of the 'seven churches of Asia' mentioned in the book of Revelation which reflects its geographical position after Ephesus and Smyrna (Revelation 1:11). Pergamum is described as the place, 'where Satan has his throne' (Revelation 2:13). This is very probably a reference to the fact that in 29 BC Pergamum became the first city in Asia to build a temple dedicated to the imperial cult worship of the Roman emperor Augustus. Pergamum was also given the title 'Thrice Neokoros', because there were three temples dedicated to the Roman emperors, in which they were worshipped as gods. Although the Roman Empire promoted polytheism, under Domitian (AD 81–96), worship of the emperor was made mandatory and a test of one's loyalty to the state.

This is probably why Antipas is specifically honoured as someone who, like Stephen, was martyred there rather than renounce his faith. The Lord Jesus, however, rebukes the Christians in Pergamum

THE THEATRE, PERGAMUM

who had indeed compromised their faith under the pressure of paganism, as Balaam had done before (2 Peter 2:15–16).

The sword was a symbol of Roman rule, so Jesus reminds them that he alone possesses the true and ultimate authority, not Rome, symbolised by his 'sharp, double-edged sword' (Revelation 2:12). The meaning of the 'white stone' (Revelation 2:17) is not certain. It is possibly a reference to a 'pebble' or tessera, used in a law court to indicate the acquittal of the accused. The new name written on it gives us assurance of our forgiveness and acceptance by the Lord Jesus Christ.

The pressure to tolerate heresy and immorality under the guise of 'alternative lifestyles' and multi-faith worship is probably as strong now as it was in Pergamum. Our responsibility is to remain pure and faithful to God alone, then we will 'overcome'. Like the manna provided in the wilderness, as we seek his strength, Jesus provides us with 'hidden manna' to sustain us (Revelation 2:17). Pergamum reminds us that no power on earth can thwart God's purposes for us if we remain faithful to our calling.

THE STAR OF DAVID FROM THE RED BASILICA, PERGAMUM

Sardis

'To the angel of the church in Sardis write: These are the words of him who holds the seven spirits of God and the seven stars. I know your deeds; you have a reputation of being alive, but you are dead. Wake up! Strengthen what remains and is about to die, for I have not found your deeds complete in the sight of my God. Remember, therefore, what you have received and heard; obey it and repent. But if you do not wake up, I will come like a thief, and you will not know at what time I will come to you. Yet you have a few people in Sardis who have not soiled their clothes. They will walk with me, dressed in white, for they are worthy.' (Revelation 3:1–4)

THE SYNAGOGUE, SARDIS

The city of Sardis was situated on the eastern bank of the Pactolus River at the southern end of the Hermus Valley, about eighty kilometres east of Smyrna and north-east of Ephesus.

The earliest settlement occupied the northern slopes of Mount Tmolus, its citadel situated on a high rocky spur, which was well fortified and easily defended. The Pactolus River, flowing at its base like a moat, ensured the city was virtually impregnable.

The wealth of Sardis was derived from gold found in the sandy shores of the Pactolus, from wool, the manufacture of textiles and jewellery. It is in Sardis that gold and silver coins were first minted by the opulent King Croesus. Due to its strategic location, as well as commercial importance on the East–West trade routes, Sardis became the capital of the ancient Lydian empire.

Ironically, because the citadel was built on such a steep, high hill, Croesus the last Lydian king, was complacent about its defence, convinced it did not need guarding. The city fell in 546 BC to Cyrus, the Persian ruler, after his soldiers observed how a Lydian descended the steep hill using steps cut into the rock to regain his lost helmet. Using this secret path the Persians entered the acropolis and captured Sardis. The people of Sardis failed to learn the lesson, because in 214 BC the city fell again, this time to Antiochus the Great who used the same tactics. Sardis is also remembered as the place from where Xerxes invaded Greece and Cyrus marched against his brother Artaxerxes.

THE TEMPLE OF ARTEMIS, SARDIS

In 334 BC, Alexander the Great captured Sardis but allowed it to remain independent. Just twelve years later, in 322 BC, it was taken by Antigonus. In 301 BC, the Seleucid kings, in turn, took the city and made it the home of their own governors. Sardis became independent again in 190 BC, as part of the Pergamum empire before eventually succumbing to Roman rule.

Sardis was also famous for its impressive Temple of Artemis as well as its mystery cults, especially one associated with Cybele. Built in the fourth century BC, the Temple of Artemis was 100 metres long and 50 metres wide, with 78 Ionic columns, each over 17 metres high. Some of these columns still remain standing today. There was also a large Jewish synagogue in Sardis, over 120 metres long and 18 metres wide. This was three times larger than any synagogue found in Palestine. An earthquake in AD 17 devastated the entire city. The emperor Tiberius gave Sardis a dispensation, freeing the city from taxation, and also helped to fund its restoration. Sardis never, however, regained its former glory.

In the first century, Sardis also had a large Christian community. It is the fifth church addressed by the Lord Jesus in the book of Revelation. The letter to 'the angel of the church in Sardis' (Revelation 3:1) suggests, however, that the church was infected with the same complacent attitude as the city. They were relying on their reputation, and failing to remain vigilant, as the city had twice failed before.

Jesus warns them, 'you have a reputation of being alive, but you are dead' (Revelation 3:1). His call to the Christians of Sardis, as to us in our day, is to 'Wake up! Strengthen what remains . . .' (Revelation 3:2). The reference to those 'dressed in white' (Revelation 3:5) would similarly have been familiar in a city renowned for its luxury clothing industry. The faithful who remain vigilant will indeed share in the triumphal coming of our Lord.

SARDIS AND THE GYMNASIUM

Colosse

Paul, an apostle of Christ Jesus by the will of God, and Timothy our brother, To the holy and faithful brothers in Christ at Colosse: Grace and peace to you from God our Father. We always thank God, the Father of our Lord Jesus Christ, when we pray for you, because we have heard of your faith in Christ Jesus and of the love you have for all the saints – the faith and love that spring from the hope that is stored up for you in heaven and that you have already heard about in the word of truth, the gospel that has come to you. (Colossians 1:1–6)

Colosse is situated on the great East–West trade route across Asia Minor where the roads from Sardis and Ephesus join, about twenty kilometres from Hierapolis and sixteen from Laodicea. The city was built over the Lycus River at the head of a gorge on one of the tributaries of the Maeander, about five kilometres from Mount Cadmus.

Two streams, one from the north and the other from the south pour into the Lycus and disappear under the city. The chalky deposits in the water have gradually formed a natural petrified arch, beneath which the current flows. This gave rise to superstitious beliefs about

angelic appearances. For instance, they believed that the archangel Michael was their protecting saint.

Colosse was a prosperous mercantile city renowned for its wool and cloth-dyeing industries from as early as the fifth century BC during the time of the Lydian and Persian empires. Xerxes, for

THE CALCIUM TAVERTINES AT PAMUKKALE NEAR COLOSSE

instance, visited Colosse in 481 BC, and Cyrus the Younger in 401 BC. The city gave its name to 'collossinus', an unusual coloured wool, probably dyed dark red or purple. By the time Paul wrote his epistle to them, however, the city had declined in influence, eclipsed by its neighbouring cities (Colossians 4:13, 16). This was in part due to the re-routing further west of the road from Sardis to Pergamum to ensure it went via Laodicea instead.

Paul had spent three years in Ephesus in which, 'all the Jews and

HONAZ DAGI MOUNTAINS BEHIND COLOSSE

Greeks who lived in the province of Asia heard the word of the Lord' (Acts 19:10). During this time Epaphras, Philemon, Onesimus, Archippus and Apphia, who were all from the region of Colosse, came to faith in Jesus Christ (Philemon 2,10, Colossians 4:9, 12). Epaphras returned to Colosse and helped found a church there (Colossians 1:7). He also ministered in the cities of Hierapolis and Laodicea (Colossians 2:1; 4:12–13). The church at Colosse met in the home of Philemon (Philemon 2). It is possible that Apphia and Archippus were his wife and son, and that Archippus was the pastor of the church (Colossians 4:17).

There was a significant Jewish presence in the area since Alexander the Great had settled Phrygia with Jews from Babylon. Cicero estimated that over 10,000 Jewish men alone lived in the Laodicea–Hierapolis–Colosse area. The distinctive features of religious life in Colosse included not only the local pagan worship of Cybele and superstitions concerning angels, but also a mixture of Jewish legalism, gnosticism and Eastern mysticism. It was this cocktail of error which Paul refuted in his letter to the young church there (Colossians 2:8–9,16–23).

Paul uses the vocabulary of the gnostic heretics, such as 'fullness', 'wisdom', 'perfect' and 'complete' but invests them with Christian meaning to describe our relationship with Jesus Christ. The little word 'all' is used thirty times to stress the pre-eminent, universal and completed work of Jesus Christ (Colossians 1:15–18; 3:11). We therefore don't have to worry about angelic mediators or legalistic practices. Colosse reminds us not to let anyone 'deceive you by fine-sounding arguments' (Colossians 2:4), that 'no-one takes you captive through hollow and deceptive philosophy' (Colossians 2:8), or 'judge you by what you eat or drink' (Colossians 2:16). We are saved by grace alone through faith in Jesus Christ.

It was Paul's hope that he would visit Colosse after his anticipated release from prison in Rome (Philemon 22). It is not known whether he did so. Shortly after Paul wrote his letter, the towns of the Lycus Valley, including Colosse, were destroyed by a major earthquake in AD 61. Although rebuilt, Colosse gradually declined in influence, increasingly overshadowed by Laodicea and Hierapolis. The legacy of Colosse is therefore not its secret rituals or prized coloured wool but the good news that everyone who believes in Jesus Christ becomes part of his body, the church, of which he is the Head (Colossians 1:18).

LYCUS VALLEY TOWARDS COLOSSE

THE SITE OF COLOSSE

Ephesus

To the angel of the church in Ephesus write: These are the words of him who holds the seven stars in his right hand and walks among the seven golden lampstands: I know your deeds, your hard work and your perseverance. I know that you cannot tolerate wicked men, that you have tested those who claim to be apostles but are not, and have found them false. You have persevered and have endured hardships for my name, and have not grown weary. Yet I hold this against you: You have forsaken your first love. (Revelation 2:1–4)

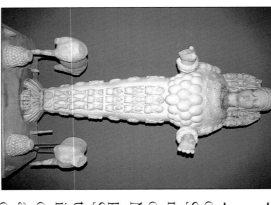

ARTEMIS STATUE, EPHESUS

Ephesus is situated at the mouth of the Cayster River, opposite the island of Samos on the west coast of what is now Turkey, between Smyrna and Miletus. Ephesus commanded a strategic location at the end of the great caravan route from the Middle East. It was also the natural point of departure across the Aegean Sea for Rome and Corinth. Ephesus therefore became the largest and most important city in the Roman province of Asia, the bridgehead between East and West. At its height the population of Ephesus is estimated to have exceeded 300,000 people. Its theatre on

CELSUS LIBRARY, EPHESUS

the side of Mt Pion seated 24,000. An artificial harbour was constructed to enable large ships to sail down the river to the city. An impressive road, 11 metres wide and lined with columns, ran from the harbour to the city, itself surrounded by a 9-kilometre wall. Ephesus was rebuilt and relocated several times on the slopes of two hills, Pion and Coressos. During the first century the harbour was already silting up so that today Ephesus is now 10 kilometres inland. This may explain why Paul met the elders at the port of Miletus (Acts 20:15–16).

The site was associated with the veneration of a grotesque fertility mother goddess which predated Greek civilisation. The worship of Artemis, as she became known in Greek, and then Diana in Latin, was influential and prosperous but degrading. Her temple, rebuilt in 356 BC after a fire, was over 140 metres long and 75 metres wide. It was open to the sky with two rows of 127 columns 20 metres high. The temple was the largest building in the Greek empire and became one of the seven wonders of the world until it was destroyed by the Goths in AD 263. The Ephesians believed the image of Artemis had fallen from heaven which suggests the

rock may have been a meteorite (Acts 19:35). Silver coins bearing the words *Diana Ephesia* found throughout Asia testify to the claim that she was indeed worshipped all over the known world (Acts 19:27). So wealthy was Ephesus, in 334 BC its inhabitants were able to decline the generous offer of Alexander the Great to rebuild the temple, if he might have his name inscribed in it. They insisted a god could not

ODEUM, EPHESUS

dedicate a temple to another god. Ephesus was also famous for its Ephesia grammata or 'Ephesian letters'. These were occult formulae written on scrolls and talismans. Furthermore, Ephesus became the centre for the imperial cult worship of the Roman emperors. With three separate temples, it qualified for the prestigious title 'neokoros' meaning 'temple warden' of the emperors, three times over.

There was also a large colony of Jews in Ephesus. Josephus, the Jewish historian, tells us that they enjoyed a privileged position, able to worship freely on the Sabbath without penalty. Paul visited Ephesus briefly, accompanied by Priscilla and Aquila who stayed on and discipled Apollos and a growing church (Acts 18:18–21). On Paul's third missionary journey he returned to Ephesus and made it his base for nearly three years (Acts 19:1–20:1). From here mission-

St. John's Basilica, Ephesus

aries such as Epaphras were sent out taking the gospel to Colossae, Laodicea and other cities in the Lycus valley (Colossians 1:6–7; 2:1). Luke could write confidently that, 'all the Jews and Greeks who lived in the province of Asia heard the word of the Lord' (Acts 19:10).

It was inevitable therefore that sooner or later there would be a confrontation between the apostles of Christ and the followers of Diana, especially those who pro-fited from her veneration, such as the Guild of Silversmiths. As people came to faith in Jesus Christ they burnt their occult scrolls and destroyed their idols. They knew

Kuretes Street, with the Celsus Library and the Temple of Hadrian

they must make a clean break with paganism. It was a costly business. A drachma was a silver coin worth about a day's wage. Luke tells us that the value of the letters burnt came to 50,000 drachmas which would have been the annual income of 150 men (Acts 19:17–20).

Because the livelihood of the silversmiths was threatened, they incited the people against Paul (Acts 19:23–34). The crowd seized Paul's companions and stormed into the stadium where they shouted 'Great is Artemis of the Ephesians' for two whole hours before the city clerk could calm them down. Paul had to be

The Roman Theatre, Ephesus

restrained from appearing. The clerk warned the mob of the serious consequences of their riot which was illegal. In so doing Luke records the official Roman judgement that Paul and the other Christians were innocent of any crime against the State (Acts 19:35–41). It is possible that Paul had this mob violence in mind when he wrote later, 'I fought wild beasts in Ephesus' (1 Corinthians 15:32).

When Paul left Ephesus, Timothy stayed behind to pastor the congregation (1 Timothy 1:3). On his return to Jerusalem, Paul arranged to meet the elders of the church in Ephesus at Miletus. He charged them to be watchful shepherds of the flock of Christ predicting that 'savage wolves' would come, even from among their own, and would lead Christians astray (Acts 20:13–38).

The Apostle John subsequently ministered in Ephesus as well. The letters to the Seven Churches of the Apocalypse were written from Patmos, a small island about 80 kilometres south-west of Ephesus, on which John had probably been exiled for his faith (Revelation 1:9). As the largest city in proconsular Asia, Ephesus is the first of the seven churches addressed. The church is praised for its intolerance of false teachers, for its hard work and perseverance. But for all that, they are rebuked for losing their 'first love'. The Lord warns them not be proud but to remember their humble origins and repent (Revelation 2:1–7).

The great city of Ephesus including its church is long gone, its harbour silted up, its people driven away by malaria, its temples empty, the worship of Artemis now ancient history. It is a sober lesson. The abiding message of Ephesus is a loving warning to every 'successful' church. It is so easy to be busy serving Christ for the wrong reasons. When we lose sight of why Christ died for us, we can lose the thrill of knowing our sins are forgiven and fail to thank him as we once did. We must never forget, as John reminds us, 'we love because he first loved us' (1 John 4:19).

THE LIBRARY OF CELSUS

Athens

While Paul was waiting for them in Athens, he was greatly distressed to see that the city was full of idols. So he reasoned in the synagogue with the Jews and the God-fearing Greeks, as well as in the market-place day by day with those who happened to be there. A group of Epicurean and Stoic philosophers began to dispute with him. Some of them asked, 'What is this babbler trying to say?' Others remarked, 'He seems to be advocating foreign gods.' They said this because Paul was preaching the good news about Jesus and the resurrection. (Acts 17:16–18)

OLYMPIAN ZEUS, ATHENS

Athens was the ancient capital of the Greek province of Attica. Named after Athene, the goddess of wisdom, it was situated about 8 kilometres from the seaport of Piraeus on the Aegean Sea. Athens was connected to the port by a road between two long walls over 80 metres apart. Surrounded by the mountains of Parnis, Pentelicus, Hymettos and Aigaleon, the Athenian backdrop is often stark and barren.

Founded well before 1000 BC, Athens became the first city to experiment with democratic government. Destroyed by the Persians in the fifth century BC, Athens was rebuilt by Pericles on an impressive scale. Using tribute money from the Athenian empire, as well as from trade and commerce, beautiful buildings were erected which centred on the Acropolis, a 170-metre high focal point of the city. The Parthenon, for example, was dedicated to the goddess Athena and contained a spectacular frieze of a great procession containing four hundred people as well as two hundred animals. The Areopagus, named after Mars, the god of thunder, was situated on a spur on the western side of the Acropolis above the Agora marketplace.

With a population of 250,000, Athens was the seat of Greek culture and learning, science and philosophy. The university became the most prestigious in the world with four great schools of philosophy – Platonic, Epicurean, Peripatetic and Stoic. It was the home of both

PARTHENON, ACROPOLIS, ATHENS

Aristotle and Plato, who founded his own Academy there in 388 BC. Socrates fared less well and was put to death in Athens in 399 BC. Even under Roman rule from 146 BC Athens continued to play an important role as the foremost university town of the empire, its influence reaching as far as Tarsus, Antioch and Alexandria.

Athens was also famous for its tolerance of religious belief, and was renowned for its temples, shrines, statues and monuments. Paul was deeply upset by this misguided religious zeal. The word Luke uses to describe the idols of Athens is found nowhere else in the Bible. It implies Athens was smothered or swamped by a forest of idols. Paul made one brief visit to Athens on his way from Macedonia to Corinth (1 Thessalonians 3:1). While there he seized the opportunity to teach and preach about Jesus Christ among the Jews in the local synagogue and also in the open air at the market place (Acts 17:17).

Areopagus is also the name of the venerable court which met to debate questions of religion and morality and authorise which teachers could lecture in public. Paul was therefore brought before the Areopagus to be examined regarding his teaching. So frequently did Paul speak of the resurrection of Jesus, they thought he was actually promoting two different gods, Jesus and Anastasis.

Despite their pantheon of gods, the Athenians had also built an altar 'to an unknown god' just in case they had missed one out. This Paul took as his starting point.

He began by identifying with them and emphasized what they could agree about God, quoting from their own poets. He stressed, however, that the one true God does not live in temples made by people, but created the whole world and revealed himself fully and finally in the Lord Jesus Christ (Acts 17:24–31). Although the Athenians did not believe in the resurrection or in a future judgement day, Paul refused to compromise his gospel and stressed both. He spoke of the facts of the resurrection of Jesus and

TOWER OF THE WINDS IN THE ROMAN FORUM, ATHENS

challenged his hearers to consider the implications for their own destiny. Our generation is very similar – dismissive of the supernatural claims of Jesus Christ yet incredibly superstitious and fascinated by the paranormal. While we must look for common ground in our evangelism we must not compromise the truth, and must make repentance and faith in Jesus Christ the issue.

It appears that only a handful of people came to believe as a result of Paul's initial ministry in Athens. However, Dionysius, a member of the Areopagus, is specifically mentioned as well as a woman named Damaris (17:34). We must not be surprised if many people will not believe our testimony either. By God's grace, some will, and in God's own good time, God will use them to lead others to himself also (2 Timothy 2:2). Our responsibility is to remain faithful to the gospel and, like Paul, God will make us fruitful.

ATHENS AND THE ACROPOLIS

Corinth

Paul left Athens, and went to Corinth. There he met a Jew named Aquila, a native of Pontus, who had recently come from Italy with his wife Priscilla, because Claudius had ordered all the Jews to leave Rome. Paul went to see them, and because he was a tentmaker as they were, he stayed and worked with them. Every Sabbath he reasoned in the synagogue, trying to persuade Jews and Greeks. (Acts 18:1–4)

TEMPLE OF APOLLO, CORINTH

C orinth is located at the western end of a narrow isthmus joining the southern Greek peninsula of Peloponnesus with the mainland to the north, about 70 kilometres from Athens. Situated at the foot of the Acrocorinth, a 566-metre hill towering over the plain below, and surrounded by a 10-kilometre wall, Corinth was easily defended and made a good fortress. The city was also blessed with two harbours, at Cenchreae, 14 kilometres to the east on the Saronic Gulf, and Lechaeum 2.5 kilmetres to the west on the Corinthian Gulf.

The isthmus at Corinth was therefore a natural land bridge between the Ionian Sea and the Aegean Sea.

Given its strategic location, dominating the North–South road as well as the East–West shipping routes, Corinth was considered the key to Greece. According to Thucydides, the first ships of war were built at Corinth in 664 BC. As early as 850 BC, the Greek poet Homer also described Corinth as a 'wealthy' city. Indeed, from about 350 BC until 250 BC Corinth became the most influential and wealthiest city in Greece, rivalling even Athens. As part of the Achaean League, however, Corinth was eventually drawn into conflict with Rome and totally destroyed in 146 BC. The Roman consul Mummius burnt the city to the ground, killing all the men and forcing the women and children into slavery. It remained desolate for over a century.

In 44 BC Julius Caesar decided to rebuild the city as a Roman colony, re-populating it with both freed Italians as well as many slaves. It soon became a vital hub within the Roman Empire and capital of the new province of Achaea, ruled by its own proconsular governor. It is estimated that in the first century, the population included 250,000 freed persons and 400,000 slaves. The famous Isthmian games were held nearby every two years bringing sportsmen, gamblers, merchants and traders to the city from all over the Mediterranean.

The wealth of Corinth was derived largely from shipping and commerce since the ports of Lechaeum and Cenchreae were connected by an overland ship-road. The cargo from large ships was transported over the narrow peninsula while smaller ships were actually hauled overland from one port to the other by a series of rollers. This enabled ships to avoid the longer and more dangerous sea route to the south around Cape Malea which was liable to severe storms in winter (Acts 27:13–20).

Although now a Roman city, Corinthians continued to worship the pagan gods of Greece. Shrines have been discovered dedicated to

Apollo, Hermes, Athena and Poseidon, the sea god. It was also a major centre for healing with a temple of Asclepius and Hygieia. Corinth was renowned, however, for its temple dedicated to Venus or Aphrodite the goddess of love. The cult of Venus had been popular in Corinth long before the city's destruction by the Romans and was revived in the new city. The temple was situated on the top of the Acrocorinth. According to Strabo, the temple was popular with sailors and brought great wealth to the city, with, he claimed, over one thousand temple prostitutes.

In a prevailing culture where immorality was the accepted norm, Corinth was especially renowned for its licentiousness. (1 Corinthians 5:1–5; 6:9–20). So much so that 'to Corinthianize' became a derogatory euphemism within Greek culture.

When Paul visited Corinth in 50 AD on his second missionary journey, it was a new and impressive but utterly depraved city. Near the centre of the city was a large marble-paved market with many shops known as the Agora. Paul mentions that the meat sold here had been dedicated to idols (1 Corinthians 8:1–13; 10:25). Nearby was the Bema, a large elevated platform with benches on three sides. It is probably here that Paul was brought before Gallio, the proconsul and brother of Seneca (Acts 18:12–18). In the residential area, archaeologists have also discovered a lintel inscribed 'Synagogue of the Hebrews' which may have been where Paul proclaimed the gospel and, when eventually rejected, founded a church next door at the home of Titius Justus (Acts 18:1–8).

Despite such a notorious reputation, where its people were poisoned by immorality and hardened by wealth and materialism, God nevertheless sent Paul, Aquila and his wife Priscilla, together with Silas, Timothy, Apollos and Titus to Corinth to preach the gospel. Paul stayed here for eighteen months and by God's grace many people were brought to faith in Jesus Christ. Paul wrote his

THE LECHAION WAY, CORINTH

letters to the church in Thessalonica as well as to Rome from Corinth and sent at least two letters back to them. The number of Latin names mentioned in Paul's letter to the Romans gives evidence of the fruitfulness of their labours there (Romans 16:21–27). These letters contain some of the most sobering as well as sublime teaching about love in the New Testament (Romans 1:18–32; 1 Corinthians 5:1–12 & 13:1–13). The controversies raised today about similar moral issues would suggest that perhaps our culture has more in common with Corinth than any other city in the New Testament. For that reason we too can take courage from the vision the Lord gave to Paul when he was tempted to give up on them, *'Do not be afraid; keep on speaking do not be silent. For I am with you, and no-one is going to attack and harm you, because I have many people in this city'* (Acts 18:9–10).

Rome

And so we came to Rome. The brothers there had heard that we were coming and they travelled as far as the Forum of Appius and the Three Taverns to meet us. At the sight of these men Paul thanked God and was encouraged. When we got to Rome, Paul was allowed to live by himself, with a soldier to guard him. (Acts 28:14–16)

Rome was the most famous city of the ancient world, synonymous with both power and empire. Situated on the Tiber River, about 30 kilometres from the Mediterranean Sea, the first settlement was on the Palatine Hill and has been dated from 753 BC. The city gradually expanded to cover the seven surrounding hills. Rome began as a monarchy ruled by kings from 753–510 BC. It then became a Republic until 31 BC when Caesar Augustus was appointed the first emperor of the Roman Empire.

In the first century AD, Rome was the largest city in the world

ROMAN FORUM, ROME

with a population exceeding one million, most of whom were slaves or plebeians. Roman citizens enjoyed 159 holidays a year, 93 of which were dedicated to sport, chariot races, games and performances sponsored by the government. The Circus Maximus, for example, could seat 200,000 people. At its height Rome contained 254 mills, 190 grain silos, 8 bridges, 8 great squares, 11 forums, 36 triumphal arches, 1,152 fountains, 28 public libraries, 2 circuses, 2 amphitheatres, 3 theatres, 11 hot spring baths and 865 private bath houses. About an eighth of the city was also laid out as beautiful parks and gardens.

Religion in Rome was essentially polytheistic. Augustus, for example, restored 82 temples in the city. Besides the traditional gods of Rome, the emperor became the focus of the empire, regarded as semi-divine while alive and achieving the status of god when dead. The imposition of the Imperial cult, the worship of the emperor, became a test of loyalty to the empire. It was because Jews and Christians refused to worship the emperor, as at Pergamum, that they came to be seen as a threat to the State (Revelation 2:13).

Priscilla and Aquila, who became co-workers with Paul in Corinth, were among the Jews expelled from Rome by the emperor Claudius in AD 49. This indicates that by this time, there was already a church in the capital although the Roman authorities did not yet appear to distinguish between Christians and Jews (Acts 18:2).

In Paul's letter to the church in Rome, written about AD 57, he expressed his desire to visit them on one of his missionary journeys, perhaps on route to Spain (Romans 15:24). Paul did indeed visit Rome three years later, but as a prisoner. He had appealed to Caesar during his trial before Festus the Roman Governor of Judea at Caesarea. Paul had been born a Roman citizen and therefore had the right to have his case heard by the emperor in Rome (Acts 22:28). Paul was confident that he and the Christian community would be vindicated from all charges brought by the Jewish authorities (Acts 25). When Paul

Both Peter and Paul were among the many Christians, mostly unknown, martyred in Rome over the next 250 years before the eventual conversion of the Roman Empire under Constantine. Jesus had taught that the best way to defeat an enemy is to turn him into a friend. Paul himself had initially been an enemy of Christ and became his friend (Romans 5:10; Colossians 1:21–22). Through Paul and the small groups of believers persecuted and scattered across the vast Roman Empire, the Lord Jesus transformed the entire world. The blood of the martyrs was indeed the seed of the church.

THE PANTHEON, ROME

landed at Puteoli, believers from Rome travelled as far as the Forum of Appius, about 70 kilometres from Rome, to welcome him. Others met them at the Three Taverns, about 55 kilometres away, to escort Paul the remainder of the journey (Acts 28:13–15). The book of Acts closes, confidently, with Paul in Rome, renting his own living quarters with a soldier to guard him. For two years he awaited his trial, free to receive visitors and proclaim, unhindered, the good news of the gospel at the heart of the Roman Empire (Acts 28:16–31). In his letter to the Philippians, probably written from Rome around AD 61, Paul gave some indication of the fruitfulness of his ministry, 'All the saints send you greetings, especially those who belong to Caesar's household' (Philippians 4:22).

In his last epistle, probably written from the notorious Marmertine Prison, Paul describes his trial. He foresees his impending death yet remains unshaken in his faith in God's sovereign purposes: 'At my first defence, no-one came to my support, but everyone deserted me. May it not be held against them. But the Lord stood at my side and gave me strength, so that through me the message might be fully proclaimed and all the Gentiles might hear it. And I was delivered from the lion's mouth. The Lord will rescue me from every evil attack and will bring me safely to his heavenly kingdom. To him be glory for ever and ever. Amen.' (2 Timothy 4:16–18)

Megiddo and the Jezreel Valley

And I will pour out on the house of David and the inhabitants of Jerusalem a spirit of grace and supplication. They will look on me, the one they have pierced, and they will mourn for him as one mourns for an only child, and grieve bitterly for him as one grieves for a firstborn son. On that day the weeping in Jerusalem will be great, like the weeping of Hadad Rimmon in the plain of Megiddo. (Zechariah 12:10–11)

Megiddo is the most strategic location in Palestine and possibly in the entire Middle East. Situated at the entrance to the main pass through the Carmel mountains, it lies on the junction of two important historic roads used by armies and traders from the Stone Age to the present day. Megiddo guards access to the Mediterranean Sea in the west and the route east through the Jezreel Valley to Damascus and Mesopotamia. The other coastal route links Egypt and Gaza in the south with Acco and Phoenicia in the north.

Control of Megiddo, therefore, has been of military importance since at least the days of Thutmose III in the fifteenth century BC right up to General Allenby's campaigns in the First World War. Jezreel, which means 'God sows' (in Greek, *Esdraelon*), separates the hills of Samaria from those of Lower Galilee. It is so flat it is possible to

see for fifty kilometres in several directions. It is easy to imagine how great armies once camped within it on twenty different occasions.

The imposing Tell at Megiddo stands 21 metres high and archaeology has revealed over twenty distinct periods of occupation.

THE NORTH GATE, MEGIDDO

THE WATER TUNNEL AT MEGIDDO

Megiddo was once one of the royal fortified cities of the Canaanites (Joshua 12:21) and before that it was of importance within the Egyptian empire. It was assigned by God to the tribe of Manasseh (Judges 1:27) but was not captured until the time of Solomon when it became one of his administrative districts (Joshua 17:11–13; 1 Kings 4:12; 9:15). During the period of the Judges the Israelites rebelled against God. He allowed Jabin the Canaanite king to oppress them for twenty years. When they cried out to God, he sent Deborah the prophetess to lead Israel (Judges 4:1–14). She inspired Barak and the northern tribes to gather near Mount Tabor to ambush Sisera and his 900 chariots. The Canaanites were defeated and Sisera came to a messy end in the tent of Jael (Judges 4:15–24).

Megiddo became one of Solomon's principal fortified cities like those at Hazor and Gezer. Extensive stables have been discovered large enough to accommodate 450 horses. These possibly date from the time of Solomon or more probably belonged to Ahab. During the divided monarchy, Megiddo again fell into the hands of the Egyptians and then to the Assyrians. In 609 BC Pharaoh Neco II and his Egyptian army passed through the Valley of Jezreel on his way to fight against the Assyrians. King Josiah ignored God's guidance and tried to resist the Egyptians at Megiddo but was fatally wounded by an Egyptian archer and died in battle there (2 Kings 23:29; 2 Chronicles 35:20–24). The prophet Zechariah, speaking prophetically, compared the mourning of King Josiah in Jerusalem with that of the crucified Lord (Zechariah 12:10–12). Summarising the importance of the Valley of Jezreel in biblical history, George Adam Smith writes, 'Esdraelon lies before you . . . the scenes of Barak's and Gideon's victories, of Saul's and Josiah's defeats, of the struggles for freedom in the glorious days of the Maccabees. There is Naboth's vineyard and the place of Jehu's revenge upon Jezebel; there Shunem and the house of Elisha; there Carmel and the place of Elijah's sacrifice . . .'

There is one brief reference to Megiddo in the book of Revelation where Armageddon means the Hill of Megiddo (Revelation 16:14–16). The Apostle John describes a great battle between the armies of the world on the final day of the Lord. It is possible that this portrays a literal battle or is perhaps a symbolic reference to the final overthrow of evil by God.

At a time when there is much foreboding about the future, Megiddo reminds us to put our hope in the sovereignty of God who rules over history, not in our intellectual genius, military strength or financial resources (Jeremiah 9:23–24).

THE STABLES, BUILT BY EITHER SOLOMON OR AHAB